The ETERNAL ROSE

"Healing an

"Inspiring"

PRAISE FOR THE AUTHOR

SARAH WEST LOVE

"Sarah's music and wisdom will heal and inspire anyone who listens!"
— *Larry Dossey, M.D. author of "Healing Words"*

"Sarah West Love gives audible life to this stillness, this possibility, both through her singing and speech. As a result, she is able to touch the deepest recesses of the heart, moving them into alignment with the world behind appearances, the world, which the greater part of humanity yearns for now as never before.

Ms. Love is in a class by herself, embodying ideals both musically and personally that situate her as a harbinger of the kind artist this planet of our demands. Fortunate indeed are those, like myself, who, having heard, knew, and having known, were forever changed. This is Ms. Love's legacy, her gift to the people of the Earth."
— *Paul Jones, concert Pianist*

"Ms. Love has a beautiful presence and talent known by millions of people all over the world. Her voice brings peace and harmony to everybody on this earth."
— *Mustafa C. Comlekcioglu*

"The one who sings is said to carry forth the torch of the light of the voice of God. For they express the spirit of the vibration of sounds within the universe, to inspire and give great upliftment to for the souls to go forth and reveal the gifts, the messages, of the "sounding of trumpets from heaven" which shall be the captains on the voyage of the new arc to freedom. Sarah West Love is the soul who has long shared her love of the One.

"Her singing transmutes separation into oneness, forgiveness replaces rage, each person feels that they are known, they are accepted, they float and fly in the love. She wants each person to know they are home. Spirits gather to bask in the glow of the angel of the infinite love."
— *Oriana*

Also by Sarah West Love

BOOKS

The Search for the Beloved
Breath of Spirit: Healing the Human Heart & Awakening to the Divine
Loving An Angel
Songs of Divinity: The Eternal Whisper
The Beloved's Tongue: The Golden Chariot
The Red Carpet: Healing wounds of SeparationI Remember Heaven
I Remember Heaven
The Golden Womb
The Golden Rose

MUSIC

Celestial Mystical Opera, Music that heals and unifies the mind, body and spirit

The Golden Solar Angel
Admission of Love
Voice of Eternity
The Sacred Pyramid
Sanctuary
Heaven
Lullaby of Peace
Sultana

SPOKEN WORD

Sacred texts and prayers written and spoken by Sarah West

The Breath of an Angel
Song of the Beloved
The Search for the Beloved
The Secret of the Beloved
The Eternal Rose

DVD

The Sound of Peace
Living Love

The ETERNAL ROSE

A Lullaby of Love for All Ages

Sarah West Love

Divine Expressions Publishing
NASHVILLE, TN • RICHMOND, VA

Copyright © 2018 by Sarah West Love

First Edition published and recorded June 1994 and appears on the authors album entitled **Voice of Eternity (1995)** orginally named **Admission of Love** (1995) and in her book **Loving An Angel** (1995).

Design by Sarah West Love and final touches with Whitney Tigani Design LLC

All Rights Reserved. Printed in the United States of America. No part of this book may be used or reproduced in any manner whatsoever without written permission except in the case of reprints in the context of reviews. The scanning, uploading and distribution of this book without permission is a theft of the author's intellectual property. If you would like permission to use material from the book (other than for review purposes), please contact permissions@SarahWestLove.com. Thank you for your support of the author's rights. For more information: www.DivineExpressionsPub.com and

Divine Expressions Publishing
4117 Hillsboro Pike, Ste 103200
Nashville, TN 37215.

Audio Book available by visiting: www.SarahWestLove.com

Library of Congress Control Number: 2018913133
ISBN: 978-0-9715751-7-2 (paperback); 978-0-9715751-8-9 (hardcover)
LS record available at https://lccn.loc.gov/
Printed in the United States of America
10 9 8 7 6 5 4 3 2 1

ATTENTION SCHOOLS AND BUSINESSES: Divine Expressions books are available at quantity discounts with bulk purchase for educational, business, or sales promotional use. For information, please e-mail the Divine Expressions Special Sales Department: SpecialSalesDEP@icloud.com.

For my Mother, my Eternal Rose,

*Thank you to my mom
whose soul is echoed in my own
My soul mate and Mama Bear,
your eternal love is the most precious
in this mortal world and throughout all time*

*I love you more than this expanding universe
and deeper than the interior
of the infinitesimally small*

*I exist because of you and all that I am
ushers forth from the spirit of eternity
where our love resides*

I love you forever

To the Creator of All Things

*To the you that remembers
to be that which you are
To the ecstasy that is life
breathing through you*

*To the transference of ecstasy
To the utterance of rapture*

*Love like it is your last time
Finally, being true to you*

*Finally,
again,
after all this time*

Finally, after all

CONTENTS

Awakening Divine Love *1*

The Eternal Rose *7*

Acknowledgments *64*

About the Author *67*

Awakening Divine Love

The profound period of time that we are in these days requires a deep opening of the Heart. We are not to just exist or coexist but to expand upon the deep pleasure of Life, of living God's Country, of being, knowing, sensing, feeling, loving what God is.

In essence the courting does not exist in that the romance began long ago and is Eternal; and therefore, in the consummation of the marriage which occurs each moment we take a breath and exhale.

We are filled with delight, ecstasy and orgasm of creation, complete and fulfilled in one "Ah–Ha", the cycle of breath; and yet, the courtship is eternal and simultaneous, even in the maturity of creation.

The Eternal Courtship is the essence. The Lovemaking seen in every luxurious breath. The Sacred Approach to every touch, glance and wish.

The innocence and wonderment are keys to the garden for in the light of the eyes of the beholder who walks with wonder and innocence is filled with utter fulfillment for there is always abundance and pleasure and no expectation other than Love. The ability to receive that Beauty. Simply by being love — becoming the reflection, what is — All that is: Beauty — that which abounds. The abundance is prolific. Look around and see God is everywhere in light and dark, shadows from the sun, gleams in the petals, the many colors, the dew dipped flowers.

In the moment of creation there is a thought that echoes out in waves upon waves.

In this lifetime as we know it, words are tools: sounds are manifestations that resonate our dreams into being and purge from us that which desires to be resolved.

Change is eminent as we beckon it forward to us, we beckon it in to our being. We consume it, swallow it, absorb it until we are saturated and can radiate it and Radiate it.

Poems — Prayers lie in the Truth of the Heart — blossoming from the soul's depths and stories. Listen for that which you know. For that which you are.

Hear that which you Remember. Acknowledge the Truth that radiates itself in these golden wings.

Hearken yourself back to God. Hearkening the You in these expressions. Hearkening the you into the hologram of wholeness. The perfect potency and reciprocation equating fulfillment.

Stand in the ship, starboard. The control room is in panorama and as you receive the information that is you, begin to feel all of you that is beyond the you that is the body. You feel the multitudes of light colors emanating multi-dimensionally sensing each tiny atom, life, knowledge, perspective and truth. This is the you that you be Now.

You are awake. Hearing the words of the wholeness of the God that you are. You expand having no limits upon receiving through the loving totality of every morsel of your being.

Love unto you. Expand is the command through release to intiation. Love.

Be Whole, readily receiving all who you are and all who you Infinitely Expand to Be.

— Sarah West Love
18 June 1994, Richmond, Virginia
City of Light

The Eternal Rose

Moments come and moments go
I hear the infinity
so far away
like in an echo chamber
passing through
Forever
The Hall of Forever

The Halls resonating
calling me
calling my name

As I sing into the Halls
into the Night
into the reverberations
that bliss me into
Being

SARAH WEST LOVE

I vibrate at the tones
forever
healing
Becoming Whole
Resonating
forever
Echoing myself
into Existence

THE ETERNAL ROSE

**God speaks
and I listen**

**I hear
Her call**

**I hear
His call**

SARAH WEST LOVE

And I surrender
I surrender
to the openness to all
that is

Welcoming me
Eternal Welcome
into the existences

THE ETERNAL ROSE

Here I Am
come find me Here
come be with me Here.

Be with Yourself
Here
into the Silences
the colors that evaporate
into Nothingness

From Blackness
into Light

SARAH WEST LOVE

From Light into Purple
Purple into Blue
Blue into Green
Green into Yellow
Yellow into Orange
Orange into Red

Vibrant
Alive
Forever
into
Black again

Cycling
cycles per second

F o r e v e r

THE ETERNAL ROSE

Welcome me
into
the Bliss of Living Joyously
I Am Here to Live
Joyously
into forever

Yes
Joyously
into Forever

I Am

I Am

I Am

THE ETERNAL ROSE

Oh,
the wind
blows
'cross my cheeks
hearing my tears fall gently
sweetly from me

THE ETERNAL ROSE

I stare out into the ocean
and I watch
the world be
created

SARAH WEST LOVE

and there is a longing still
still

THE ETERNAL ROSE

Remembrance of a time when there
was Nothing
except God
created in blackness
before the stars

before the Galaxies
before the Infinite expansion
that appears as
a retraction

SARAH WEST LOVE

Before God felt the pain
of being
not God
before the Heart felt separate
from its maker

I remember
I remember this
so sweetly so Divinely
We were all whole
we were forever

    and we knew it

THE ETERNAL ROSE

SARAH WEST LOVE

We knew our selves

We knew the all

We knew the One

SARAH WEST LOVE

Oh, and we felt every ounce

every molecule

every quark

THE ETERNAL ROSE

We were
and we were
aware of All things

Oh, and we loved each other so
Oh, and we loved ourselves
Oh, so Beautifully

Come to Now and Remember

Remember This
Remember
when we were all
whole

We were all one
and we loved
so deep

We were only but Love
We were all Love

Nothing else
All Love

All expansion
All humility
All knowing through Love
such utter Love

I call back now a Remembrance
of This
into the entire Universe

Every ounce of Our Being
Remembers This

Remember
Become it again
that which you
always have been

THE ETERNAL ROSE

Hear me
Oh, God
Hear Me

Remember the Divinity
that we are

I Am

SARAH WEST LOVE

I count the Petals on the Rose
and I see her blossoming
Velvety Gross Beauty
for finer than that is Our Essence
beyond Vision

                the Unfolding of Creation
                there
                In the Heart

                I Am

The Big Bang
is the Love in the heart
when the heart opens
and Creation emerges
All every where

It felt
the Love emerge

The blossoming of the Heart.
the true rose of Forever
the refinement I Am

The red fragrance and the Velvet
tongue of the Petals

THE ETERNAL ROSE

Oh, that is I
that is I
caressing my cheek
with such eternal spirit
with the fragrance
of the deepest Love
and the deepest profundities
the deepest sacredness
the deepest awareness

I Am the Rose

calling

SARAH WEST LOVE

THE ETERNAL ROSE

SARAH WEST LOVE

I said a prayer today

to call in the God force knowingness

to bring in

the awareness

of tranquility on Earth

in all of ourselves

It is Here

the Peace that

We Seek

the wholeness that we long

it is Here

THE ETERNAL ROSE

It is Here
Right now
in Me

I beckon it to me
and become it
again

That which always has been Me
I beckon it and it Is

I become it
Glowing Infinitely
I Rise

SARAH WEST LOVE

I Rise
into the Light
in the beam
of the shaft of Light
that I stand in
that is me

that is where I Belong
that is my Home

It is the place of Creation
from which I stand
It is the place from which
we all stand in our own beams

THE ETERNAL ROSE

Back to God

Becoming God

Becoming the Light Source

that We Are

It is through us from us

Becoming Us

It is all that we are

Remember

SARAH WEST LOVE

Remember This

Remember

what it's like to stand

in connectedness

of All Things

THE ETERNAL ROSE

Recall the imagery of wholeness
of Fullness of God
of Fullness of the Mother
Cradling of the Father
warming

and the child
You Are All These

The Creator and the Created

THE ETERNAL ROSE

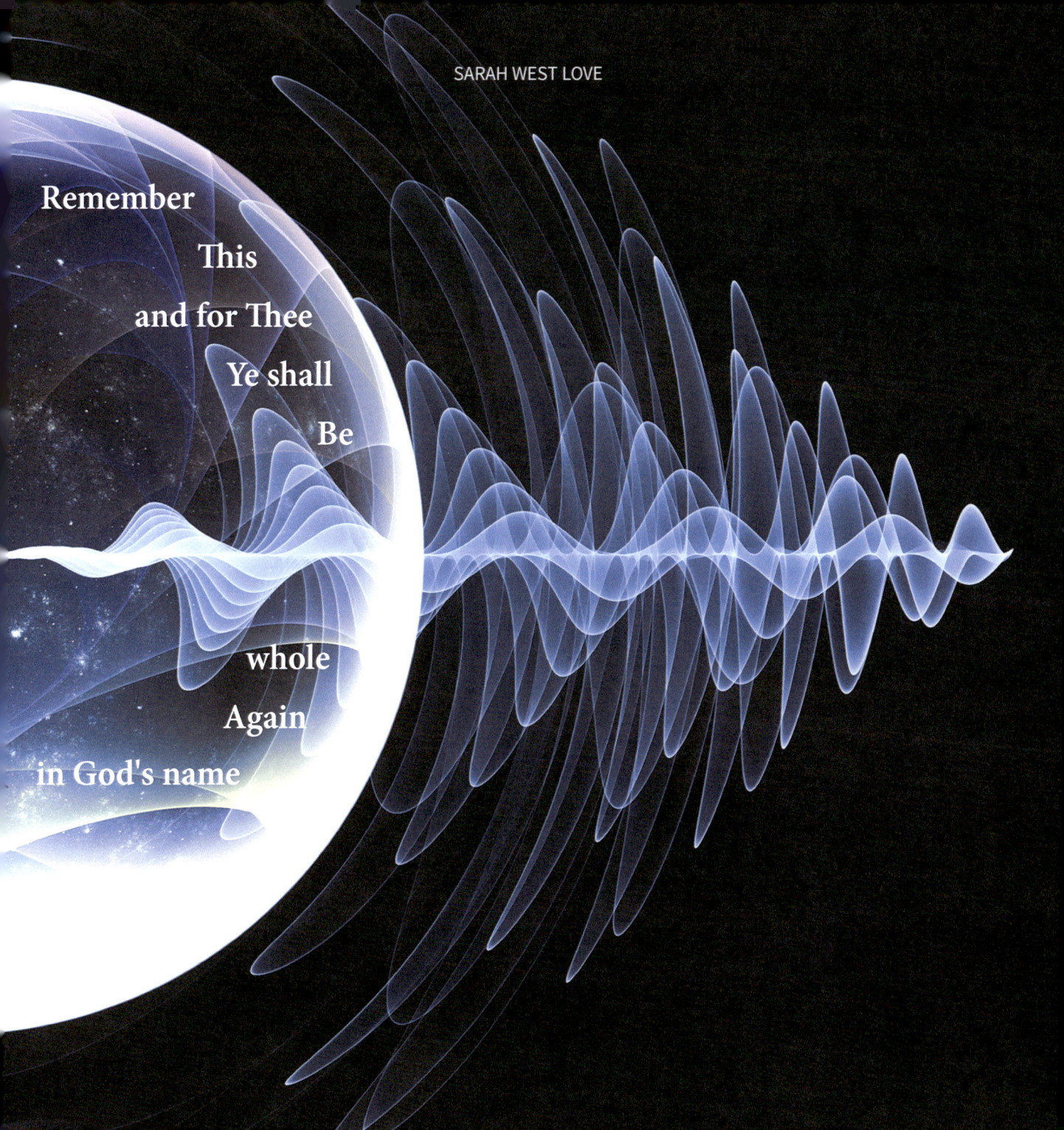

THE ETERNAL ROSE

In the Light of the Mother

In the Light of the Father

SARAH WEST LOVE

In the Light of the Holy Daughtron

In the Light of the Holy Son

THE ETERNAL ROSE

SARAH WEST LOVE

Purchase the MP3 audiobook of

THE ETERNAL ROSE:
A Lullaby of Love for All Ages

where they are sold online and on Ms. Love's website:

www.SarahWestLove.com

ACKNOWLEDGMENTS

Thank you to Andrea Post for her depth of caring and passion for the words residing in these pages. Your love and encouragement inspired me to dig deep to create what you see now: this book reborn in this beautiful format decades later for a new generation in this critical time for humanity. I am so grateful for your sacred tenderness and keen spirit. How profoundly blessed I am to stand near your effulgent loving heart.

Thank you to Whitney Tigani for helping me put the final touches on my book. Your exquisite craft elevated my design with your generous spirit and impeccable eye that I feel in every part you touched. I am in awe of your gift and in awe that I found you right in time. What a miracle you are.

SARAH WEST LOVE

Thank you to Kevin Kravitz. I am grateful for your friendship over all these years. Your uplifting presence and profound heart is lifesaving.

About the Author

SARAH WEST LOVE

Sarah West Love is an internationally renowned composer, performer, author, film-maker, artist, healing facilitator, teacher, speaker, podcast host, TV producer and psychic. Ms. Love offers Celestial Mystical Opera Concerts, Quantum Healing Workshops & Psychic Sessions throughout the world. Her most recent book & CD includes *The Search for the Beloved (Book of Love Vol. II)*. Learn more on her website: **www.SarahWestLove.com**

INSTAGRAM: @SarahWestLove

FACEBOOK: /SarahWestLove

TWITTER: @SarahWestLove22

INSTAGRAM: @BookOfLove.shop

MUSIC & BOOK CATALOG

FOR

SARAH WEST LOVE

Music for Awakening your Healing

&

Enlivening Your Genius:

Creativity, Relaxation, Massage, Sleep & more

Order Online:

www.SarahWestLove.com

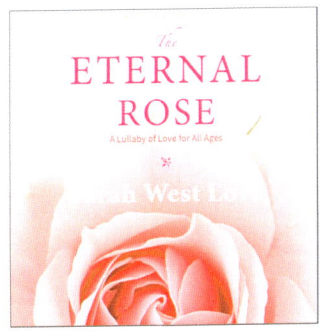
THE ETERNAL ROSE
BOOK/CD

SEARCH FOR THE BELOVED
BOOK/CD

TRAIN OF FREEDOM
CD

LULLABY OF PEACE
CD

SULTANA
CD

LOVE
CD

SANCTUARY
CD

THE SACRED PYRAMID
CD

VOICE OF ETERNITY
CD

www.ingramcontent.com/pod-product-compliance
Lightning Source LLC
Chambersburg PA
CBRC090058020526
44112CB00030B/61